A Short History
of the Short Story:

Western and Asian Traditions

Gulnaz Fatma
MA, MBA, PhD (Pursuing)

From the World Voices Series

Modern History Press

A Short History of the Short Story: Western and Asian Traditions
Copyright © 2012 by Gulnaz Fatma. All Rights Reserved.

From the World Voices Series

Library of Congress Cataloging-in-Publication Data

Fatma, Gulnaz.
  A short history of the short story : Western and Asian traditions / Gulnaz Fatma.
    p. cm. -- (World voices series)
  Includes bibliographical references and index.
  ISBN 978-1-61599-166-2 (trade paper : alk. paper)
  1. Short story. I. Title.
  PN3321.F38 2012
  809.3'1--dc23
                            2012027290

Modern History Press, an imprint of Loving Healing Press
5145 Pontiac Trail
Ann Arbor, MI 48105
USA

www.ModernHistoryPress.com
info@ModernHistoryPress.com
Tollfree 888-761-6268

Distributed by Ingram Book Group, Bertrams books (UK).

Contents

Acknowledgments	i
Preface	ii
Chapter 1 - The Short Story: An Overview	1
Chapter 2 - Chief Elements of a Short Story	4
Chapter 3 - Principal Reasons for the Short Story's Popularity	10
Chapter 4 - The Development of the Short Story	12
Chapter 5 - The Short Story in America and Europe	18
Chapter 6 - The Short Story in India	23
Conclusion	32
Bibliography	34
About the Author	36
Index	37

Acknowledgments

I would like to thank my supervisor, Professor Iffat Ara, for her esteemed guidance and patience. She has always been supportive and encouraging and has fostered my academic growth. I would also like to thank all members of the Department of English at Aligarh Muslim University, especially the Chairperson, Professor S. Nuzhat Zeba, for her cooperation in my research. I extend a special thanks to my parents, Mr. Mahboob Hasan and Mrs. Shahnaz Begum, and to Mr. Mahmood Hasan, Shamanaz, and Mahnaz for supporting me at every step of my life.

Finally, I would like to thank my dear friend Mohd Aarif Khan for providing careful and critical readings and challenging me to think more critically.

I owe my profound thanks to Tyler R. Tichelaar, editor of this book, for his keen interest and worthy guidance. His critical reading of my book enabled me to form a conceptual framework of this book.

Last, but not least, I would like to thank to Victor R. Volkman, the Senior Editor of Modern History Press, for publishing the book in such a beautiful form and in a timely way.

Preface

In this book, I have tried to present a brief and clear account of the short story in the literature of the East and the West. I have attempted to provide wide references to short story literature, with full bibliographical details. My intention has been to produce a book in simple form for the use of college students, research scholars, and for such readers as might be interested in knowing the short story's historical background.

I hope my endeavor will be found useful. Any suggestions for this book's improvement will be most welcome.

Gulnaz Fatma
MA, MBA, PhD (Pursuing)
Aligarh Muslim University
Aligarh, India
May 26, 2012

Chapter 1 - The Short Story: An Overview

The short story is one of the oldest types of literature, and it has existed in many forms, including myths, fairy tales, ballads, and parables. The modern short story, in an improved form, originated in the first quarter of the nineteenth century first in the United States of America. Before the short story came into existence, different genres of literature had been popular in different periods. For example, in the sixteenth century, drama was the dominant form of literature, and in the eighteenth century, the essay was the center of interest, but in the nineteenth century, these forms lost much of their popularity as novels and short stories replaced them.

The short story took a long time to reach its modern form. It was very much influenced by the novel because it is a miniature form of that art of prose fiction. It is difficult to trace the earliest form of prose literature because with the passage of time, many forms of literature lost their identity and the process of change gave them an altogether new appearance.

A short story sometimes contains little or no dialogue, but it may also be made up of dialogue while the description is brief, as in Stevenson's collection *Island Nights' Entertainments* (1893) where local color is dominant. A modern short story describes all kinds of problems. In Washington Irving's "The Stout Gentleman" (1822), a whimsical fancy is worked out with admirable skill. Poe's "The Gold-Bug" (1843) is based on a puzzle, Stevenson's "Olalla" (1885) is an excursion into morbid psychology.

H.G. Wells describes the purpose and art of the short story as:

> The jolly art, of making something very bright and moving; it may be horrible or pathetic or funny or profoundly

Chapter 2 - Chief Elements of a Short Story

The modern short story, regarded today as being its own genre of literature, has deep roots. Short stories that necessarily teach a moral lesson are associated with parables or fables. These particular forms of the short story have long been popular with religious and spiritual leaders as a way to teach; they used them to inspire and enlighten their admirers. In earlier times, such stories were precise, their purpose being primarily to illustrate some moral or spiritual truth.

The same brevity and truth is present in the short story today. The short story is supposed to be more straightforward than a novel because it contains a smaller number of incidents, plots, and characters, spread over a shorter span of time. In lengthier fiction, the story has dramatic overtones such as an exposition or introduction of the setting, the situation, the main characters, and the conflict represented in decisive moments that build up to the climax for the protagonist, as well as a resolution that often has a moral drawn from the story. The short story, however, because it is short, does not necessarily follow this pattern. For instance, modern short stories rarely have an exposition.

Short stories typically have an abrupt beginning or succeed in being short by beginning in the middle of the action. In long short stories, the plot may also have a climax, crisis, or turning points. Short stories may also end abruptly, and they may imply a meaning or theme without discussing a moral lesson. Also, the short story changes itself according to the writer's mood.

Professor Bliss Perry of Harvard has thrown light both on the advantages and limitations of the short story form. He is of the opinion that both novelists and short story writers attract their readers' attention by presenting "Certain persons doing certain things in certain

Edgar Allan Poe

circumstances" (Matthews 40). Both writers create characters, plot, and settings; however, short story writers have limited scope and time, so they present very few characters and dare not concentrate much on character development; therefore, very few experiences are taken into account. The central character in a short story is an imposing figure. If situations are more important than characters, then character development is simpler. The heroine of Frank Stockton's "The Lady, or the Tiger?" (1882) is an ordinary woman, and the hero of Edgar Allan Poe's "The Pit and the Pendulum" (1842) is also a plain man. The situation presented attracts the reader's attention. In a short story, often the character becomes more important than the plot, although the plot may be the impetus for the character to become a more important person. If the author concentrates on settings, he will ignore and get on well without character and plot. The setting and atmosphere will be made to appeal to the reader, who becomes absorbed in the surrounding scenery. The modern reader may be attracted by the story's landscapes, social situations, and the world of nature, which inspires them. When the short story writer opens up new horizons, such as writing about war, commerce, or industry, he or she inspires readers to see the world and life in new ways and thereby attains popularity.

It is pretty hard to draw a line of demarcation between a short story and other forms of fiction. A classical way to define a short story is that it should be able to be read in one sitting. This viewpoint was expressed by Edgar Allan Poe in his essay "The Philosophy of Composition" (1846). A simple way to define a short story is to adhere to a certain length. The Science Fiction and Fantasy Writers of America, in its Nebula Award for Science Fiction submission guidelines, defines a short story as having less than 7,500 words. In general, length definitions for short stories may run from 1,000 to 20,000 words. Stories under 1,000 words are usually called "short short stories" or "flash fiction." Stories over 20,000 words are typically novellas, while novels will have more than 40,000 words.

The short story, like the novel or drama, also has a theme and characters, but the structure of a short story is significant because the number of incidents it contains all center on the main and usually only plot, which the reader retains in his mind. The short story has only flashes of description and few characters. A character is not portrayed fully, and a single incident usually completes the story. Hence, the short story is considered as a one man story today.

Ancient prose forms like the folktale and the myth are difficult to absorb today. Myth is essentially a religious term and is, therefore, as old as religion, but with the passage of time, the myth lost its relevance. New scientific developments have rendered meaningless a belief in myths. The legend is a crude form of myth and has greater resemblance to the short story. Both are old and formerly quite popular forms of short stories. Similarly, the fable is an early form of short story, in which animals and birds are the characters and moral lessons are taught.

Writers of short stories have certain limitations because, along with brevity, there should be clarity of expression. The story should keep the reader in a state of suspense, and instead of teaching a moral lesson or imposing any belief on the reader, the story should leave the reader free to judge characters, events, and situations in light of his own

William Shakespeare

understanding and common sense. Hence, unity of purpose and effectiveness of expression make the story more acceptable to the reader.

In ancient times, prose was the common vehicle of amusement and reformation. When short stories were first written in English, many were translations from Italian or ancient sources, or borrowed freely from them to create their own stories or versions of earlier stories. Some stories told of early times in history, especially in England or America, while others were tales of voyagers, and yet other authors wrote of the present day.

The short story is intoxicated with language. Early short story writers employed a generous, flowing, and melodious style. Writers were almost writing in a new tongue because during the Renaissance, English had been enriched beyond all recognition by borrowings from ancient and foreign authors. And the new writers of the sixteenth and seventeenth centuries used this increased language for their benefit. The writers made full use of language while poetic forms taught them economy, so when writing prose, their writing gained simplicity and vigor.

During Elizabethan times, authors and readers loved a highly decorative mode of expression both in prose and poetry. The maxims and sentences of advice for gentlemen were quoted and admired in the court. We find this excellence in the works of William Shakespeare (1564-1616) and other writers who were influenced by him. The use of antithesis and alliteration was in vogue. The character in a play or poem spoke in long monologues and in lengthy and multiple sentences, which for today's readers is monotonous and tedious. References to classical literature were in fashion, such as a discussion of friendship making an allusion to the biblical David and Jonathan, or a reference to faithlessness containing an allusion to Cressida. This wealth of classical allusion was used to decorate pages that dealt with matters of everyday experience.

By the late seventeenth century, however, a more direct poetic style came into existence with poets like John Dryden (1631-1700); this style then influenced the creation of a smooth, simple, and vigorous kind of prose that became fashionable in English literature for the first time. Soon, thereafter, the first fictional prose works, the earliest forms of the novel, appeared, including John Bunyan's *The Pilgrim's Progress* (1678), Daniel Defoe's *Robinson Crusoe* (1719), Jonathan Swift's *Gulliver's Travels* (1726) and Samuel Richardson's *Pamela* (1740). The popularity of these longer novels eventually led to the shorter form of the short story by the beginning of the nineteenth century with American writers like Washington Irving (1783-1859), Edgar Allan Poe (1809-1849), and Nathaniel Hawthorne (1804-1864).

Since the short story originated, writers have given a new form to the short story, making it supple, extending its scope by using it for their own purposes, and providing readers with excellent specimens of narrative skill, thus making it superior to the Greek myth, which had "A lack of variety in its themes, a lack of interest in its treatment and a lack of originality in its form" (Matthews 4). In a short story, the author was free to do what he liked with the relations of the characters.

While early short story writers often used supernatural elements, by the end of the nineteenth century, a focus on realism became dominant in the short story form. In this art, there was nothing too far-fetched, nothing too sentimental, no sorrows too unreal. Hence, short story writers such as Giovanni Verga (1840-1922) in Italy, Alexander Lange

Kielland (1849-1906) in Norway, and Ivan Turgenev (1818-1883) in Russia, used this perfect form, creating stories with unity, simplicity and harmony, variety and originality. They applied all these elements to the life around them with which they were well-acquainted. They gave to the short story a richness of content and brought it close to life and its realities. Their works advanced the form beyond what earlier writers like Poe had done because they concentrated more on the construction of plot than characterization.

Today, it is difficult to define a short story for various reasons. A number of writers have used this form of art so it has been experimented with in multiple ways. Its form and contents are beyond imagination. The short story contains all sorts of situations, episodes, and various types of talent. Hence, opinions are sharply divided on the nature and characteristics of the short story. Like all forms of art, it uses experiences of everyday life to a higher level. The short story, in the hands of a modern master, is a perfect work of art. The modern short story writer is an artist, who is a close observer of life, a keen student of character, and a master of style. Every subject between heaven and earth is now regarded fit for the short story, and it can be told in any manner that may please the artist and his or her readers.

Chapter 3 - Principal Reasons for the Short Story's Popularity

Numerous causes have led to the short story's development as a popular form of literature. The rapid development of the short story in modern times is largely due to the hectic schedule of life that does not allow people to devote enough time to reading the lengthy epics, novels, and plays that appealed to earlier readers. Now, people can hardly afford to read lengthy novels like Henry Fielding's *Tom Jones* (1749) and Samuel Richardson's *Clarissa* (1748), the latter the longest novel in the English language at roughly 2,600 pages, because it takes a long time to read fiction continuously. Modern readers want to read short stories for recreation so they can forget the worries of the world for a while and relax after a hard day's work. Furthermore, the short story can be read quickly in one sitting; it does not require careful perusal or a second reading to understand it, as might a poem. For these reasons, the short story has attracted readers' attention and become a popular form of literature.

The modern short story first came into vogue with the growth of journalism, resulting in its publication in all types of magazines and journals. While the short story first became popular in the United States of America as an effort to create a distinct form of American literature separate from European styles, its popularity quickly grew in Europe. The reason for the short story's popularity in Europe was twofold; the more alert writers accepted the classicist code of unity and proportion, and it gained the hospitality of Parisian journalism, which had always been close to literature. The French do not publish many magazines, perhaps because their newspapers have enough scope in them for artistic appreciation and their readers often logically felt everything they needed they could find in these publications. The daily journals of Paris were the first to publish most of the short stories of Fromental Halévy (1799-1862), Jean Richepin (1849-1926), and François Coppée (1842-1908). And whenever the list of the world's most admirable short stories is prepared, it definitely contains more than one of the amusing fantasies of Alphonse Daudet (1840-1897).

While the short story flourished in the United States and France in the nineteenth century, it was not given due weight during this time by the well-known British men of letters, for various reasons, including that Poe was viewed as excelling all others as the writer who gave a perfect form to the short story for the first time. Also, in England, the magazines tended to publish serialized novels, which could not obtain such popularity in America in that format. Furthermore, the large English reading public had a variety of interests, which they did not feel American fiction could fulfill, and the English tended still to see their writers as superior to American authors.

Following the age of Irving, Hawthorne, and Poe, American short story writers began to give local color to stories as well as to indulge in humor, sentimentality, feminist themes, and realism. Northern and Southern writers in the United States differed in their forms of sincerity and their presentations due to the size, variety, and different experiences of the American people. They described people of all kinds and introduced readers to their fellow citizens in other parts of the country, thereby broadening their outlook. In no other country had such an exploration relating to contemporary humanity been achieved—perhaps because in no other country could such an experiment of multiculturalism have succeeded.

Alphonse Daudet

Chapter 4 - The Development of the Short Story

Short stories began with the oral storytelling tradition, which led to the composition of epics such as Homer's *Iliad* and *Odyssey*. These oral narratives were based on rhythmic verse, which included Homeric epithets; such stylistic devices served the purpose of mnemonics, which made the memorization of the story an easier task. Short stories in the form of verse laid emphasis on individuals' narratives, which were related hurriedly.

The refined form of the short story emerged from various developments relating to this genre, such as brief tales having a moral, as asserted by the Greek historian Herodotus who, in the sixth century B.C., first narrated the tales of a Greek slave named Aesop, although other interpretations relating to his country and age are also given. These ancient stories came to be known as *Aesop's Fables*.

Fables typically were stories of animals who could talk and who resembled human beings in many other respects; although *Aesop's Fables* were written down, most fables were stories related orally, and they continued to be narrated by one generation to the next. These oral legends and beast fables were both long and precise, with beast fables gaining the greatest popularity. From this collection of fables, Bidpai and Aesop selected stories, which were improved by refined narrative artists such as Jean de La Fontaine (1621-1695), whose collected fables were didactic and satiric in spirit.

Every fable contains a moral, even though it is not necessarily found at the story's end. The ethical aspect highlighted by the storyteller in an animal story can be found in the medieval European fables of Reynard the Fox, or more recently in the Br'er Rabbit stories of *Uncle Remus* (1881) collected by Joel Chandler Harris from African-Americans in the Southern United States. A very apt moral is also present in Rudyard Kipling's *The Jungle Book* (1894), where the writer describes Mowgli's growth to manhood in the company of Nature. These beast fables are entertaining and reflect the artistic skill of the author, who is sensitive about the changing aspects of life. However, such beast fables only have a slight resemblance to a short story.

Another early short story form popular in medieval Rome was the anecdote. The anecdote resembled parables with a realistic narration that provided food for thought. These Roman anecdotes were compiled in the thirteenth and fourteenth centuries, and were known as *Gesta Romanorum*. The anecdote was popular in Europe until the eighteenth century, influencing such works as the anecdotal fictional depiction of Sir Roger De Coverley, a character in English authors Addison and Steele's publication *The Spectator* (1711).

Other early brief tales that are considered precursors to the short story are tales of supernatural background. Many of these stories were Egyptian narratives, such as "The Tale of the Two Brothers" (circa 1200 B.C.) and "The Story of the Shipwrecked Sailor" (circa 1600-2000 B.C.), which exist on ancient papyrus manuscripts. Also some supernatural stories were found in the pages of Herodotus (484-425 B.C.), who was primarily a historian but gifted with the art of storytelling.

Surprisingly, the Greeks, during their period of decline, were more inclined to write prose, while during the height of their glory they found expression through poetry; none of the nine muses were ever assigned any task relating to the composition or inspiration of prose fiction. The best brief stories in Latin, such as Petronius' "The Matron of Ephesus" in his *Satyricon* (1st century A.D.) with its satiric ingenuity, attracted the attention of modern poets who adapted the tales in their own style.

Because the novel became the dominant literary form in the nineteenth century, it is noteworthy that novels often contained short stories within them. Miguel de Cervantes' *Don Quixote* (1605 and 1615) contains one minor narrative that merely expanded his novel without improving it; similar experiments were made by Paul Scarron in *Le Roman comique* (1651-1659), Henry Fielding in *Tom Jones*

Miguel de Cervantes

(1749), Charles Dickens in *The Pickwick Papers* (1837), and Sir Walter Scott in *Redgauntlet* (1824), where we find "Wandering Willie's Tale," a fine specimen of Scott's humor and fancy; this story is better presented in the larger romance by the same author, and it reads like an anticipation of a real short story found rarely in the history of the novel. Many special characteristics of the short story could also be found in the novelettes of this time, including originality of theme and ingenuity of invention, but they lack the short story's brevity. The late Locker Lampson is of the opinion that Pope's narrative poem "The Rape of the Lock" (1712) would be the best possible example of a short story during this period because of its narrative perfection, despite its irrelevant length. Similarly, the best of the novelettes, such as Greek author Longus' *Daphnis and Chloe* (2nd century A.D.) translated into French by Jacques Amyot in 1559, must be distinguished from the more compact short story.

In Europe, the oral storytelling tradition transitioned into written stories during the late Middle Ages, most notably with the publication of Giovanni Boccaccio's *Decameron* (circa 1350-1353) and Geoffrey Chaucer's *Canterbury Tales* (circa 1386-1393). Both these works consist of individual short stories written in narrative form (a framework of stories). In the sixteenth century, a very popular set of darkly tragic stories were written by Matteo Bandello (c.1480-1562) which may be precursors to the novella.

In mid-seventeenth century France, the novella was developed by authors such as Madame de Lafayette (1634-1693). In 1704, Antoine Golan's first modern translation of *The Thousand and One Nights* or *The Arabian Nights* also had a great influence on the eighteenth century development of the European short story and early writers such as Voltaire (1694-1778) and Diderot (1713-1784). Other forms of oral tales similar to *The Arabian Nights* began to be collected and published in the early nineteenth century, such as the Brothers Grimm's *Fairy Tales* (1824-26) and Nicolas Gogol's *Evening on a Farm of Dikanka* (1831-32). The tales that perhaps led to the emergence of a modern short story in the United States were Charles Brockden Brown's "Somnambulism" (1805), and Washington Irving's "Rip Van Winkle" (1819) and "The Legend of Sleepy Hollow" (1820).

In the later nineteenth century, with the publication of the print magazines and journals, short-fiction consisting of about 3,000-15,000 words came into vogue. Famous short stories of this period include Boleslaw Prus' "A Legend of Old Egypt" (1888) and Anton Chekhov's "Ward No 6" (1892). Also in the same period, the first literary theories relating to the short story became popular. A well-known literary theory for the short story was developed, beginning with Edgar Allan Poe's essay "The Philosophy of Composition" (1846). In 1901, Brander Matthews, the first American professor of dramatic literature, published the short book *The Philosophy of a Short-Story*, thereby naming the short story genre.

In the first half of the twentieth century, a number of scholarly magazines such as *The Atlantic Monthly*, *The New Yorker*, *Scribner's Magazine*, and *The Saturday Evening Post* published short stories in each issue. Because short stories were popular and monetary gains were equally good, writers like F. Scott Fitzgerald (1896-1940) frequently turned to short story writing. Even Brander Matthews preferred to write short stories to pay his many debts.

After World War II, literary short fiction gained great popularity in the United States. *The New Yorker* regularly published the short stories of mid-century writers like Shirley Jackson, whose well-known story "The Lottery" (1948) spoke to the history of the times. Other major short story writers of this time include John Cheever, John Steinbeck, Jean Stafford, and Eudora Welty. J.D. Salinger's *Nine Stories* (1953) represented new thinking, while Flannery O'Connor's *A Good Man Is Hard to Find and Other Stories* (1955) represented the Southern Gothic style. When *Life* magazine published Ernest Hemingway's long short story or novella *The Old Man and the Sea* in 1952, 5,300,000 copies of the issue were sold within two days.

Cultural and social life would affect the short fiction of the 1960s. Philip Roth and Grace Paley seemed to represent the Jewish-American spirit of that era. Tillie Olson's "I Stand Here Ironing" highlighted a feminist perspective. James Baldwin's "Going to Meet the Man" was a story about African-American life. Frank O'Connor's *The Lonely Voice* (1963) was the first major examination of the short story form and highly influential. In the 1970s, the post-modern short story was developed in the works of Donald Barthelme and John Barth, and in the same decade, Pushcart Press, a publishing house established by Bill Henderson, began publishing the best work of lesser quality presses and sponsoring its Pushcart Prize along with publishing an anthology of the winning stories.

Shirley Jackson

Stephen King, one of the most popular novelists of recent decades, began his career by writing and self-publishing short stories in fanzines. In his fifth short story collection, *Just After Sunset* (2008) he wrote:

> The novel is a quagmire that a lot of young writers stumble into. I started with short stories and I got comfortable with that format and never wanted to leave it behind. (Brook and Warren 177)

In the 1980s, minimalism—an effort to depict the essence of something by removing all non-essential forms—gained influence and affected the works of short story writers such as Raymond Carver, Ann Beattie, and Bobbie Ann Mason, while traditionalist American authors like John Updike and Joyce Carole Oates also continued to produce short stories as did Canadian author Alice Munro. John Gardner's *The Art of Fiction* (1983) became a seminal reference text for how to create short fiction and continues to be used in university creative writing programs.

Many of the American short stories of the 1990s are examples of realism. Several prominent writers, such as Tim O'Brien in his collection of related short stories *The Things They Carried* (1990), dealt with the legacy of the Vietnam War. Louise Erdich wrote effectively about Native American life. T.C. Boyle and David Foster Wallace highlighted the psychology of popular culture practitioners; others who wrote in this style included Steven Millhauser and Robert Olen Butler. Stuart Dybek became known for his presentation of life in Chicago's refined neighborhoods.

The first years of the twenty-first century have seen the emergence of a new group of young writers, some of the best known being Jhumpa Lahiri, Karma Russell, Nathan Englander, Kevin Brock, George Saunders, and Dan Chaon. Blogs and ezines have emerged and joined traditional paper-based literary journals in publishing the works of short story writers and bringing them to the public's attention.

Chapter 5 - The Short Story in America and Europe

The short story first developed as a modern literary form in the United States and France in the mid-nineteenth century. American writers had for the first time almost given a perfect form to this genre. Right from their onset, the newly published magazines had to rely for their popularity mainly on the short stories they printed. While novelists in England typically published their work in the form of lengthy serials, certain factors in the United States, such as a vast country and diverse population with varied interests, prevented the American novel's development and popularity from exceeding the short story form. Novels that provided more detailed studies of American life were not published until much later in the nineteenth century, examples being Mark Twain's *Huckleberry Finn* (1884) and William Dean Howells' *The Rise of Silas Lapham* (1885).

Most American writers thought it more convenient to express themselves through short story writing; it enabled them to write more freely about the parts of the country they knew well and to present a smaller number of characters with specific characteristics. Short stories relating to everyday experiences in the United States were suitable for the time. Irving wrote "Rip Van Winkle" (1819) by creating characters built off of legends. Hawthorne exercised a more abiding influence because, although using historical settings, he reflected the spirit of the age through his writing. The short story reached its perfection in the hands of Edgar Allan Poe, who received great fame with the publication of "An MS Found in a Bottle" (1833). Poe holds his readers' attention with the skill of his narration and the atmosphere he creates. His influence on modern short story writers cannot be underestimated.

Charles Dickens

In Great Britain, the short story was slow to establish itself, and for many years, narrative art was not associated with short story writing. Writers preferred to convey their thoughts and experiences through novels because they provided more scope and brought fame to their authors. The London magazines and weeklies did not entertain short story writers and preferred the publication of long serial tales, which assured the circulation for a year. For example, the periodical *The Argosy* (1865-1901) was launched with the serialization of Charles Reade's novel *Griffith Gaunt*. Of course, Charles Dickens is the best known author of the period who serialized his own and other authors' novels in his periodicals *Household Words* and *All the Year Round*. The latter saw the serialization of Dickens' *A Tale of Two Cities* (1859) and *Great Expectations* (1860-61) as well as Wilkie Collins' *The Woman in White* (1859-60).

Brief tales were written and published in English magazines, but these were not up to the mark and were authored by less reputed writers. British writers and the reading public were the last ones to develop a taste for short story writing and give it an equal status with novels, so they did not benefit from this form of writing until well after their French and American colleagues. The British flare for short stories would finally manifest in the works of Robert Louis Stevenson (1850-1894) and Rudyard Kipling (1865-1936), both of whom had been influenced by Poe and other American short story writers. Stevenson had a certain spiritual closeness with Hawthorne, disclosed most clearly in "Markheim" (1884), one of the world's most powerful and beautiful short stories. Kipling contributed a number of worthwhile short stories including "Without Benefit of Clergy" (1891), "The Brushwood Boy" (1898), and "They" (1904). While the British were sluggish in contributing to this new form, when two of their best known authors tried the form, they won fame as remarkable short story writers. The late nineteenth and early twentieth century saw several other masters of the short story in Britain, including Sir Arthur Conan Doyle, John Galsworthy, H.G. Wells, and Somerset Maugham.

From America, the short story passed to Europe. In France, acknowledged masters of the short story were Honore Balzac (1799-1850) and Guy de Maupassant (1850-1893), and in Russia, Anton Chekhov (1860-1904) and Leo Tolstoy (1828-1910). All these authors are acknowledged for the grace, wit, and charm in their stories.

After Irving and Hawthorne, a large number of American writers made experiments with short story writing, reflecting local life of the times through their characters. These included humorists, sentimentalists, lovers of fantasy, realists, and people belonging to all parts of the country. With the passage of time, the scope of writing widened and readers became acquainted with all sorts of people and knew them better through the works of authors.

Poe was the first writer who admired the art of story writing and preferred it to tale-telling, which was too lengthy. Professor Perry has thrown light both on the advantages and limitations of short story writing by stating that unlike in the novel, the writer gets an opportunity "for innocent didacticism, for posing problems without answering them, for stating arbitrary premises, for omitting unlovely details and conversely, for making beauty out of the horrible, and finally, for poetic symbolism" (Matthews 42). Also, a good short story requires the author to have a developed visual imagination and an ability to select the required details; because the short story is brief, it deals with a fleeting moment in a character's life so consistency is not required as it is in the novel with its long and continuous presentation.

In the United States, Hawthorne and Poe had a predecessor in Irving, whose happy tales, despite their lack of restraint, are accepted as the earliest model of the short story. If one is very particular about the form's definition, one is bound to remove the name of Irving from the list of the short story's originators. Irving did not sacrifice his attractive imaginative thinking at the cost of compression and a straightforward way of putting things. He loved to linger on and get approval from his readers through his narrative style. Irving possessed all the characteristics of a good short story writer, including inventiveness and imagination, but he did not care for unity and swift compactness, which became standard in the works of Hawthorne and Poe and are now a requirement. These are the essential qualities which are discerned in "La Vénus d'Ille" (1837) by Prosper Mérimée, written in France soon after the publication of Poe's "Bernice" (1835). Both Mérimée (1803-1870) and Théophile Gautier (1811-1872), earned fame in short story writing by exhibiting their artistic impulse, which was quite spontaneous and thereby seemed to be in accordance with the genre's theory. While Poe excelled Hawthorne in his artistic aim and conception of what a short story ought to be, Hawthorne was a more richly endowed artist.

Nathaniel Hawthorne

In a review of Hawthorne's tales, Poe first precisely mentioned the principles relating to the art of short story writing; they are still often highlighted because they are regarded as authentic by some of the best short story writers in every modern language. After Poe had given a definite form to the short story and made it more receptive, it could develop on its own with the assistance of modern writers. It was no doubt different from the novel, as lyric is different from the epic. It could achieve perfection not by mere chance but by deliberate and resolute effort. Like the sonnet, the short story had to abide by certain rules, yet its limitations encouraged the true artist to follow the technique and thereby enhance his talent by working within the form. The short story also satisfied writers who did not want to choose a more difficult or longer form.

In a tale or short story based on an incident, emphasis is laid on the consequences relating to events, as in Edgar Allan Poe's "The Gold-Bug" (1843) and other detective stories, in the stories of O. Henry (1862-1910), and in the stock adventure stories published by magazines in the nineteenth and twentieth centuries. Stories of character throw light on the state of mind, motivation, psychological and moral qualities of the protagonists. In quite a few of the stories of character by Anton Chekhov, everything is based on an encounter and conversation between two people—two waiters will reveal everything through their mutual conversation. In some stories, interest is maintained between external action and character; Hemingway's "The Short Happy Life of Francis Macomber" (1936) is full of incidents of violence and resembles a sensational adventure tale, but the details of action and dialogue are meant to test and reveal the characters, along with a number of reversals that reflect the inherent attributes of the three protagonists.

In modern literature, some writers of the short story achieve excellence by enlarging its scope, making it suitable to their purposes, and offering readers their own language in beautiful short stories. For example, in Italy, Giovanni Verga (1840-1922) made good use of this perfect form, benefiting by its unity, simplicity, and harmony and giving it variety, interest, and originality. Such short story writers describe the life around them, the lives of their own countrymen, and the life they know best, thus giving the short story a human touch that Poe never would have imagined since his ultimate aim was construction rather than character delineation.

Chapter 6 - The Short Story in India

In India, the short story in its earliest form as tales and myths was quite popular from ancient times. Then during the British rule of India, Indian-English prose writing arose and was first associated with translations as well as political agitation, social reform, propaganda, law and education. Over time, from this mix arose a new literature of Indians writing in English. Today, Indian-English literature is popular and fashionable in India and Indian writers of English have achieved fame worldwide. These writers have received literary laurels because of their perception, vision, articulation, depth, variety of topics, and their universality of appeal.

Indian writers have successfully experimented with the short story form and narrative techniques. Some well-known writers who have received recognition are R.K. Narayan, Mulk Raj Anand, Rabindranath Tagore, Raja Rao, Manohar Malgonkar, Salman Rushdie, Anita Desai, Arun Joshi, Shashi Deshpande, Ruskin Bond, Shiv K. Kumar, Khwaja Ahmed Abbas, Dina Mehta, Farrukh Dhondy, Ruth P. Jhabvala, Indu Suryanarayan, and Manoj Das. They have all written a large number of stories, and they are known for their depth of perception, the subtle expression of their experiences, their style, variety, and innovativeness. And yet, these short stories have received little critical attention, in India or abroad, despite their being so well-known.

In *A History of Indian Literature*, Sisir Kumar Das, in describing the short story in India, states:

> There are at least three distinct stages in the growth of the short story as a modern form. All these stages are autonomous and self sufficient but interrelated. (Das 302)

These three stages are anecdotes, tales and fables, and short fiction. The third stage, according to Das, emerged during the nineteenth century with the publication of journals and periodicals. These periodicals led to the development of character sketches and frequency of incidents and ultimately to the short story. Das makes a very apt statement in this regard:

> The short story distinct from anecdotes, tales, sketches, reportage and novellas came at the last stage of the evolution of narratives. As a form, it shares some features of these four but it developed its own distinctiveness identified by the presence of a conscious narrative, foregrounding a particular incident or a situation, or a moment of emotional intensity. (Das 302)

Since India is a storehouse of tales and parables, when the printing press started, these stories first appeared in printed form with certain modifications. The short story as a literary genre was used in all Indian languages, in particular when mythological, adventurous, and marvelous stories had less appeal and the novel had come into existence. In different regions, the short story was called by various names, such as: Katha, Akhyan, Upakhyan, Afsana, and Dastan. Short stories appealed to both children and adults. The Vedas, Upanishads, Puranas, the Panchatantra and Hitopadesha, and Jatak Kathas became a storehouses of tales that provided material to the writers.

Mr. Rama Rao refers to India's literary history and its influence on the short story in modern Indian literature thus:

> We have had in India stories which lie embedded in hymns of the *RigVeda* or scattered in the *upnishad* and the epics, the stories which constitute *panchtantra*, *Hitopdesha*, *Dashkumarcharitra*, The Buddhist Jatak Kathas in Pali and a host of similar stories in modern Indian languages. (Rao 216)

Indian prose writing is as old as humanity itself, while the English short story form is only about two hundred years old. Indian writers in English have been using almost all major forms of literature, but the short story has received a great deal of practitioners.

Rabindranath Tagore

As in the United States, Indian short story writers chose their form of art because through this medium, they could explore India's multifaceted aspects of life, and through journals and publicity, a widespread audience could be reached. The common man played a vital role in the development of the modern short story because common men and their lives and problems became the focus of attention in a short story. Hence, the short story as a means of portraying everyday life and its affairs became very popular. Rabindranath Tagore (1861-1941) seems to have shown the first sign of maturity in the Indian short story because:

> For the first time in modern Indian literature, the life of ordinary men and women received such sympathetic understanding and was depicted with such love and feeling. (Das 307)

Tagore's stories were an example of the distinctiveness of the form, and both writers and readers recognized them as being more mature and superior to stories that had been written previously.

The description of the common man in a story played a vital role in the development of the short story in India. The short story portrays the common man with all his problems so that the themes were universal. The short story, therefore, acted as a balance between historical novels and novels dealing with social problems by identifying a new zone of experience. The short story was closer to the novel in its early stages, but after some time, it more closely resembled the lyric in its compactness of form and unity of emotion while presenting life in a modernized way. The first Indian to give the short story this modern look was Fakir Mohan Senapati in his short story "Lachamania" (1868).

Because the common reader relished a complete story in one installment, instead of a serialized novel, short stories were frequently published in journals and periodicals. Thus in India also, the journals and periodicals played a crucial role in making the short story quite popular. Indian short story writers preferred the short story form not because of any special interest in it, but because they found the form to be quite simple and because it was the most popular means to present Indian life as its writers saw it. Hence, the writer primarily concerned with conveying an idea, or wanting to disseminate eternal values and truth as perceived by Indians, would choose the short story as his medium.

Soshee Chandra Dutt in London published the earliest collection of Indian short stories entitled *Realities of Indian Life: Stories Collected from Criminal Reports of India* (1885). In the same year, Dutt and Sourindra Mohan Tagore published together *The Times of Yore, or Tales from Indian History*. Soon after, P.V Ramaswami Raju presented two collections *The Tales of the Sixty Mandarins* (1886) and *Indian Fables* (1887), from London. In the nineteenth century, two more writers of anthologies came upon the scene, namely, Kshetrapal Chakravarti who published *Sarala and Hingara: Tales Descriptive of Indian Life* (Kolkata, 1895) and Samuel and Kamala Satthianadhan, who published *Stories of Indian Christian Life* (Madras, 1898). B.R. Rajam Aiyer's stories appeared in the *Prabuddha Bharata* during 1896-1898, and then were published in the anthology *Rambles in Vedanta* (1905).

Despite these collections, not many short stories appeared before the beginning of the twentieth century. Cornelia Sorabji, who was an advocate in Kolkata, was the first Indian short story writer with impressive work to her credit. She produced four short story collections: *Love and Life behind the Purdah* (1901), *Sun-babies: Studies in the child-life of India* (1904), *Between the Twilights: Being studies of India women by one of themselves* (1908), and *Indian Tales of the Great Ones Among Men, Women and Bird-People* (1916). Other significant short story anthologies of the period were S.M. Natesa Sastri's *Indian Folk Tales* (1908), Dwijendra Nath Neogi's *Sacred Tales of India* (1916), A. Madhavia's *Short Stories*, written under the pseudonym Kushika (1916), and Maharanee Sunity Devee's *Bengal Dacoits and Tigers* (1916), *The Beautiful Mughal Princess* (1918).

Most of the late nineteenth and early twentieth century short stories of India resemble folktales, legends, and parables. They are simple in their art, tending to be anecdotes, sentimental, and didactic. The Western short story considerably influenced Indian writers during this time with several European writers becoming known to Indian readers through translations. The early Indian writer faced several serious obstacles so far as his creative art in English was concerned. He had to adapt the English language to his needs and motives to portray effectively contemporary India to his readers, so less effort was made to experiment with technique. Early Indian short story writers were not as concerned with the individual and his personal problems; instead, characters tended to be types rather than individuals, often representing the different social classes. English education was becoming popular and Western writers set a model for portraying social scenes effectively. The publication of periodicals also helped Indian writers to develop their prose style.

After 1920, the Indian short story in English reached its zenith. At this time, Shanker Ram wrote his short story collections *The Children of Kaveri* (1926) and *Creatures All* (1933). His later stories present the rural life of India. He uses literal translations of rustic utterances like "Barrel Nose Grandpa." He presents the superstitions, the caste system, the poverty, and other rural problems of India during his era.

Social reform was one of the major concerns of writers at this time, called the Gandhian Era when Gandhi was promoting freedom for India from British rule. During this period, A.S.P. Ayer's *Sense in Sex and Other Stories* (1932), K.S. Venkataramani's *Jatadharan* (1937), and K. Nagarajan's *Cold Rice* (1945), among many other short stories, deal with social reforms in society. Writers during this time often seem ambivalent in their attitude to the tension resulting from the conflict between traditionalism and modernity. At the same time, they highlighted the ancient Indian values of service, sacrifice, non-attachment, and dedication to a moral cause.

During this period, the Indian creative mind became critical about Indian traditions and some short story writers started to assert the Indian ethos in their works. S.K. Chettur throws light on rural superstitions, feuds, and the concept of the supernatural in his short story collections *The Cobras of Dhermashei and other stories* (1937) and *The Spell of Aphorize and other stories* (1957).

The most famous writers of this period, Mulk Raj Anand, Raja Rao, and R.K. Narayan, depicted the cultural clash, which was prevalent, and it was closely examined in their creative works.

Anand's collections are *The Lost Child and other stories* (1934), *The Barber's Trade Union and other stories* (1944), *Reflections on the Golden Bed and other stories* (1947), *The Power of Darkness and other stories* (1959), *Lajwanti and other stories* (1966) and *Between Tears and Laughter* (1973). Anand employs a variety of narrative modes. His stories reveal various moods, persons, social surroundings, and colors of life. Even his style varies remarkably; his stories are like fables, parables, and folktales. The stories also reflect Anand's reformative zeal and his psychological inquiry. Anand's stories attack the hypocrisy of the people. He sympathizes with the lower classes in society and shows their lot, due to social injustice and the strong prejudices exhibited by the privileged communities. He satirizes the irrational and often inhuman customs of the feudal society. He also attacks evils like child marriage, patriarchy, untouchability, lack of sanitation, and cruelty in society.

R.K. Narayan's collections include *Dodu and other stories* (1943), *Malgudi Days* (1943), *An Astrologer's Day and other stories* (1947), *Lawley Road and other stories* (1956), and *A Horse and Two Goats* (1970). Narayan presents reality in a lighter vein. His stories end happily. He comically reveals the truths of life, yet he does not allow cynicism or mockery to enter the world of his creations. He reveals the ironies of life impressively.

Raja Rao depicts philosophically the Indian reality with its focus on the social and political aspects of life. He makes profound use of folktales, myths, and legends. He has a profound vision of life and is deeply rooted in his Indianness. Rao's stories are highly symbolic and philosophical. Among his best works are *Kanthapura* (1938), *The Cow of the Barricades and Other Stories* (1947), *The Serpent and the Rope* (1960), *The Cat and Shakespeare: A Tale of India* (1965), *Comrade Kirillov* (1976), *The Policeman and the Rose: Stories* (1978), *The Chessmaster and His Moves* (1988), and *On the Ganga Ghat* (1989).

Manjeri Isweren (often spelled as Isvaran in English) is an enjoyable short story writer with nine collections to his credit, including *Rickshawallah* (1946) and *Painted Tigers* (1956). His focus is the lower and middle class people in south India in general and Tamil Nadu in particular. He writes about war, the Indian struggle for freedom, the innocence of children, the problems of women, and social evils. Isweren's depiction of women is commendable. He shows how families come under the influence of traditionalism and modernity and the consequences relating to this situation.

After India achieved independence, the vision and perception of many writers changed because now they were facing a new situation. Making a new India was the main concern of all. Hence dreams, promises, and plans for a better India form the major theme of many short stories and other works of literature at this time.

Among the later twentieth century Indian short story writers is Khushvant Singh, whose four short story collections are *The Mark of Vishnu and Other Stories* (1950), *The Voice of God and Other Stories* (1957), *A Bride for the Sahib and Other Stories* (1967), and *Black Jasmine* (1971). He too attacks hypocrisy. R.P. Jhabvala, a daughter of Polish parents, was born in Germany and educated in England. Because she was married to an Indian, she lived in India for more than two decades; apart from eight novels, she published the short story collections *Like Birds, Like Fishes, An Experience of India* (1966), *A Stronger Climate* (1968), and *How I Became a Holy Mother* (1976). She keenly observes Indian life and its social mannerisms.

Today, Ruskin Bond and Manoj Das are the prominent contemporary Indian short story writers in English. Ruskin Bond has brought out a number of collections of short stories, including *My First Love and other stories* (1968). Manoj Das has written *The Crocodile's Lady: a Collection of Stories* (1975) and *A Little Night Music* (2004). Many more names can be added to prepare a bibliography of short story writers of modern India. These authors write about contemporary life in India and about Indians living abroad.

In its initial stage, the Indian short story was like the occasional diversion of a novelist. Hence, it was not up to the mark. The formative phase of the short story, by writers such as Tagore, whose stories were written in Bengali and translated into English, was one in which originality of conception and craftsmanship were missing. Dwivedi states of such early Indian short stories:

> Their propensity for social amelioration and moral instruction blinds them to the inherent charms of the art of story-telling. There is a general lack of vision and artistic sense. (Jain 124)

However, with its increased popularity and perfection, the short story has made us aware that it is better to examine its possibilities and limitations than to try to define it in precise terms. Short story writer Manjeri Isweren is also a critic or theorist of the form. He expressed his views on the short story in "By Way of Preface" to his book *A Madras Admiral* (1959):

> A short story can be a fable, or a parable, real or fantasy, a true presentation or a parody, sentimental or satirical, serious in intent, or a light-hearted diversion. (Isweren 217)

In 1966, Mulk Raj Anand commented on the significance of the short story genre during this time in these words:

> And when the history of Indian culture comes to be written in the next century, it may appear that the inmost longings, thwarting of the many peoples of our country, as expressed in the short-stories, are more authentic evidence of the life of our time than the slogan of politics and the very obvious outer events. (Anand 132)

However, the Indian English short story, despite the flexibility of its form and its publication opportunities, has failed to achieve its own identity. A.N. Dwivedi aptly says that the critics have treated it casually (Jain 124). Although a powerful and distinct form, today, the short story remains often considered as a byproduct of the novel.

Conclusion

The short story, unlike the novel, must be precise. The effects of the novel and the short story are also different. Edgar Allan Poe may be regarded as the founder of the short story genre and its first critical theorist. He recommended that, "The prose tale as a narrative can be read, within a short time." Regardless of all the elements and forms of short stories, Poe's remark remains relevant because of the precision and tightness required by the form. As a result, the short story writer presents few characters because a detailed analysis is not possible, and therefore, unlike the novelists, the short story writer must remain within his or her limitations. The author has to rush to the climax. The prior exposition and the details, relating to the setting, and additional complications must be avoided and the denouement must be summed up quickly. The central incident must hurriedly reflect the life and character of the protagonist. All other details are reserved for an impressive development of the plot. This precision often creates a greater effect in a good short story than the artistry found in an elaborate novel because of its loose structure.

Of course, many famous short stories do not follow this pattern. Hence prose fiction has many forms as well. The short story that consists of perhaps five hundred words is different from such long and complex forms as Herman Melville's *Billy Budd* (1891), Henry James' *The Turn of the Screw* (1898), and Thomas Mann's *Mario and the Magician* (1929), all works that are really novellas because they are between the tautness of the short story and the expansiveness of the novel.

Generally, stories cannot be truly considered "short stories" if they run beyond fifty pages. Short stories are commonly classified as around five to twenty pages, but as mentioned, they alter by length depending on their authors. Therefore, longer stories that cannot quite be called novels are considered "novellas," and like short stories, they are commonly placed into the economically wise choice of an anthology or story collection that frequently contains previously unpublished stories.

Sometimes, authors who do not have much time or money to write a novella or novel decide to write short stories instead of writing a novel. The short story is still viewed as a practice ground for writers who might later write a novel, and writing short stories is a way to begin a writing career. But there is no doubt the short story is a form in itself that deserves special attention and recognition.

Bibliography

Abrams, M.H. *A Glossary of Literary Terms*. Banglore: Prison Books, 1993.

Allen, Walter. *The Short Story in English*. Oxford: Oxford UP, 1981.

Anand, M.R. "Introduction." *Comparative Indian Literature*. Vol. 2. Ed. K.M. George. New York: Macmillan, 1966.132-133.

Bates, H.G. *The Modern Short Story from 1809 to 1953*. London: Robert Hale, 1988.

Brooks, Cleanth and Robert Penn Warren. *The Scope of Fiction*. New York: Appleton Crafts, 1960.

Cuddon, J.A. *A Dictionary of Literary Terms*. New Delhi: Clarion Books, 1980.

Das, Sisir Kumar. (ed.). A History of Indian Literature: 1800-1910: Western Impact, Indian Response. New Delhi: Sahitya Akademi, 1991.

Gelfant, Blanche and Lawrence Graver (eds.). *The Columbia Companion to the Twentieth-Century American Short Story*. New York: Columbia UP, 2000.

Hart, James (ed.) *The Oxford Companion to American Literature*. Oxford, Gr. Brit.: Oxford UP, 1995.

Isweren, Manjeri. "The Role of The Story Teller in the Modern World." *The Aryan Path*. Dec. 1957. 216-217.

Kempton, K.P. *The Short Story*. Cambridge: Harvard UP, 1954.

Magill, Frank. (ed.) *Short Story Writers*. Pasadena, CA: Salem Press, 1997.

Matthews, Brander. *The Philosophy of The Short Story*. New York: Longmans, Green, 1901.

Mundra, J.N. and C.L. Sahani. *Advanced Literary Essays*. 4th Edition, Braeilly: Prakash Book Depot, 1965.

"A Study of Prose Fiction," by Bliss Perry, Chapter XII, *The Short-Story*, pp. 300–334. Boston and New York: Houghton, Mifflin & Co., 1902.

Rao, M. Rama (ed.). "The Short Story in Modern Indian Literature." *Fiction and the Reading Public in India*. Mysore: Mysore UP, 1967.

Shaw, Valerie. *The Short Story: A Critical Introduction*. London: Longman, 1983.

"Short Story." *The New Encyclopaedia Britannica*. 15th ed. Micropaedia vol. 10. Chicago: Encyclopedia Britannica, 1998.

Summer, Hollis (ed.). *Discussions of the Short Story*. Boston: Heath, 1963.

Venugopal, C.V. *The Indian Short Story in English: A Survey*. Bareilly: Prakash Book Depot. 1976.

Ward, A.C. *Twentieth Century Literature*. London: Methuen, 1992.

Watson, Noelle (ed.) *Reference Guide to Short Fiction*. Detroit: St. James Press, 1994.

About the Author

Gulnaz Fatma is an Indian writer and author. She is a research scholar in the Department of English at Aligarh Muslim University in Aligarh, India. Fatma is a dynamic personality in literature studies who has published many articles in national and international journals. She is the author of a grammar book published by KGA Publications, and she is currently writing a novel on the themes of immigration and multiculturalism.

Index

Aesop, 12
Afsana, 24
Akhyan, 24
Anand, Mulk Raj, 30
anecdote, 13
anthology
　use of, 33
Bengali, 30
Boccaccio, Giovanni, 14
Bond, Ruskin, 23, 30
Brown, Charles Brockden, 15
Bunyan, John, 8
Cervantes, 13, 14
Chaucer, 14
Chekhov, Anton, 2, 15, 20, 22
Chettur, S.K., 28
Das, Manoj, 23, 30
Dastan, 24
Daudet, Alphonse, 11
Deshpande, Shashi, 23
Dryden, John, 8
Dutt, Soshee Chandra, 26
Dwivedi, A.N., 30, 31
fables, 4, 12, 23, 28
Fielding, Henry, 10, 13
flash fiction, 6
folktale, 6, 27
Gandhian Era, 27–28
Gautier, Théophile, 21
Harris, Joel Chandler, 12
Hawthorne, Nathaniel, 8, 11, 18,
　20, 21

Hemingway, Ernest, 16, 22
Henry, O., 22
Herodotus, 12, 13
India
　war of independence, 29
　western influences, 27
Irving, Washington, 1, 8, 11, 15,
　18, 20, 21
Isweren, Manjeri, 29, 30, 34
Joshi, Arun, 23
Katha, 24
Kathas, Jatak, 24
Kipling, Rudyard, 13, 20
local color, 1, 11
Madhavia, A., 27
Maugham, Somerset, 2, 20
Maupassant, Guy de, 20
Mérimée, Prosper, 21
Narayan, R.K., 23, 28
novella
　defined, 6
periodicals, 19, 24, 26, 27
Perry, Bliss, 4, 20, 35
Petronius, 13
Poe, Edgar Allan, 1, 2, 5, 6, 8, 9,
　11, 15, 18, 20, 21, 22, 32
　and Hawthorne, 21
　as founder, 32
　Bernice, 21
　vs. Verga, 22
Raju, P.V Ramaswami, 26

Rao, Raja, 23, 28, 29
Richardson, Samuel, 8, 10
Rushdie, Salman, 23
Shakespeare, 7, 8, 29
short story
  length, 6
  rules of, 22
  types of, 20
Singh, Khushvant, 29
Stevenson, R.L., 1, 20

Stockton, Frank, 5
Tagore, Sourindra Mohan, 26
Tamil Nadu, 29
Upakhyan, 24
upnishad, 24
Venkataramani, K.S., 27
Verga, Giovanni, 8, 22
Walpole, Hugh, 2
Wells, H.G., 1, 3, 20
Welty, Eudora, 16

www.ingramcontent.com/pod-product-compliance
Lightning Source LLC
Chambersburg PA
CBHW061306040426
42444CB00010B/2547